# WATERFAll TO AGILE

A PRACTICAL GUIDE TO
AGILE TRANSITION

# WATERFALL TO AGILE

A PRACTICAL GUIDE TO
AGILE TRANSITION

ADE SHOKOYA

*Foreword by Agile Manifesto Author*
ARIE VAN BENNEKUM

TAMARE
HOUSE

The right of Ade Shokoya to be identified as Author of this work has been asserted in accordance with sections 77 and 78 of the Copyright, Designs and Patents Act, 1988.

First published in Great Britain with TamaRe House, August 2012
25 Brixton Station Road, London, SW9 8PB, United Kingdom
+44 (0)844 357 2592, info@tamarehouse.com, www.tamarehouse.co.uk

Proofreading services by Kwemara Publications

Copyright © Ade Shokoya, 2012

No part of this book is to be reproduced, reprinted, copied, or stored in retrieval systems of any type, except by written permission from the Author. Parts of this book may however be used only in reference to support related documents.

All rights reserved.

A CIP catalogue record for this book is available from the British Library.

This publication employs acid free paper and meets all ANSI standards for archival quality paper.

ISBN: 978-1-908552-23-5

## Dedication

*To my beautiful rock Mabel and ray of light Kaiyan*

*Thank You x*

# Contents

Acknowledgments .................................................... XI

Foreword ............................................................. XIII

Preface ................................................................. XV

1 Beware of the Lion That Inherited the Wrong Kingdom .................................................................. 1

2 Beginning with the End in Mind ............................... 6

3 The Starting Point .................................................... 10

4 If You Don't Know This Then Your Agile Transition Is Likely to Fail ......................................... 14

5 The Secret Ninja Weapon That Leads to Organisational Change ............................................. 23

6 How to Eat an Elephant ............................................ 27

7 Doing This Will Help You Stand Out ...................... 30

8 How to Influence People by Tuning into the World's Favourite Radio Station ............................... 34

9 Six Sure-Fire Ways to Get People to Agree with You ............................................................................ 38

| 10 | The Thing That Motivates All Human Behaviour - and How to Use It to Your Advantage | 43 |
| 11 | Without This All Your Hard Work Will Come to Nothing | 48 |
| 12 | How to Avoid a Common Mistake That's Sure to Leave Your Agile Transition Dead in the Water | 53 |
| 13 | Do This and You'll Have Everyone's Cooperation | 59 |
| 14 | The Key to Succeeding with Agile | 62 |
| 15 | Doing This Only Takes a Minute, but the Results Can Last a Lifetime | 65 |
| 16 | How to Build Effective Agile Teams | 70 |
| 17 | How to Quickly Cut Through Red Tape and Avoid Frustrating Bureaucracy | 76 |
| 18 | What to Do When Things Go Wrong | 79 |
| 19 | A Rule of Thumb Worth Bearing in Mind | 83 |
| 20 | What You Need to Know about Agile Best Practices | 86 |
| 21 | The Oak and the Reed | 89 |
| 22 | The Truth about Agile | 92 |

23  The Bigger Picture ...................................................... 95

   About the Author ..................................................... 100

WATERFALL TO AGILE

# Acknowledgments

I would like to express my gratitude and appreciation to the many people who have contributed to the ideas in this book, as well as all those who have given me the support needed to complete it:

To Arie van Bennekum for mentoring me, answering my many questions and guiding me through some of my biggest Agile transition challenges.

To Jeff Sutherland for the 'light bulb' moment that led to a broader understanding of what Agile is.

To Ron Jefferies for helping me to see the commonality between the Agile methodologies.

To Mary & Tom Poppendieck for showing me the importance of applying Lean-Agile concepts at the organisational level.

To Ester Derby, Jeff Patton and the many other Agile experts I have spoken to over the years for sharing their Agile transition experience and knowledge with me.

To the team at SQE Training (Kim Bryant, Alison Wade, Lee Copeland and Holly Graham) for providing me with exclusive interview access to world leading Agile experts from Google, Microsoft and other multi-billion dollar corporations.

To my loving fiancée, Mabel for giving me honest feedback and supporting me in writing this book.

And finally, to my son Kaiyan for being my inspiration.

# Foreword

Over ten years ago Agile was defined as the umbrella expression for the different methods presented during the Snowbird event in February 2001. I think none of the authors of the Agile Manifesto (myself included) ever imagined what the role of the concept and the word Agile would become during the next decade.

The first moment I realised this was during the Agile Conference celebrating the ten-year anniversary in 2011 in Salt Lake City where I met so many people living, dreaming, and breathing Agile. One of those people was Ade Shokoya.

Since then we have met multiple times, at meetings in warm and sunny Salt Lake City and also in the snowy, frozen, and traditional Netherlands. During those meetings, we had many discussions about what it takes to successfully transition from a non-Agile organization and environment to an Agile one. Based on our conversations, I became impressed by Ade's work, his views, his approach, and his future ambitions.

One of Ade's future ambitions was writing a book on the transition process from non-Agile to Agile in organizations, and here it is. Read it, digest it, and use it to guide you in achieving your transitional objectives. I know you'll enjoy it.

**Arie van Bennekum**
(co-)author of the Agile Manifesto
#arievanbennekum
arie@pmtd.nl
www.agileinthecore.com

# Preface

The fact that you're reading this right now more than likely means you recognise that Agile practices enable companies to benefit from quicker returns on investment, cut costs, gain a competitive edge, and better align IT needs with business objectives. However, despite all these benefits, surprisingly many people are still finding it hard to convince senior management and customers (who might have been working in the Waterfall way for many years) to adopt this alternative approach to software and product development.

Part of the problem is that even though there is a lot of available information about Agile, the majority of it focuses on Agile theory and not Agile in practice. And we all know, theory doesn't always work in practice. So although the books, blogs, webinars, etc., might be able to tell you how to do Scrum, Kanban, or XP, what they don't do a good job of is helping you create the organisational and cultural environment essential to the successful implementation and execution of the different Agile methodologies. As a result, transitioning from Waterfall to Agile is proving difficult for many people who can see the potential benefits Agile has to offer but are struggling to get "the powers that be" on-board. Understandably, this can become very frustrating. And the constant struggle leaves you feeling like you're banging your head against a brick wall, fighting an uphill battle, and can even cause you to sometimes doubt yourself.

But the truth is, it doesn't have to be that way. You don't have to experience all that frustration, pain, and stress. Because, with proven techniques and strategies, you will be able to create a successful Agile transition that will give you more influence in your organisation and greater control over your career. You will also benefit from greater job security, quicker promotions and a much higher income. All you need is the right information, guidance, and support to help you create those results.

As you know, the global economy is very volatile at the moment, and things aren't looking like they will get better any time soon. Across Europe and America unemployment is at an all-time high, and the predictions are that more people will lose their jobs over the coming years. However, as more and more organisations transition from Waterfall to Agile, those individuals with the knowledge and experience that will enable organisations to maximise the benefits they get from Agile practices (e.g., reduced development costs, quicker returns on investment, improved quality, and a greater competitive advantage) are the ones who will benefit from greater job security (at a time when people are struggling to hold onto their jobs), get promoted quicker (at a time when people are being made redundant) and get paid more (at a time when wages are going down and people are struggling financially).

## PREFACE

You see, a few years ago Forbes carried out research into the factors that contribute most to some people being made redundant while others aren't. And what they found is that the people who are closest to the income stream of an organisation (i.e., the people whose contribution and work directly translates into some form of income or cost savings for the business) are the ones less likely to lose their jobs – and in the unlikely event they do get made redundant during economically turbulent times, they tend to get hired very quickly by somebody else.

So, if Agile offers such a great opportunity on both a personal and organisational level, why aren't more people successful with it?

Well, the truth is, most people are not committed to learning what it takes to overcome the obstacles involved with Agile transition. They are all for it when things are going smoothly, but when they encounter the inevitable issues they are sure to face along the way, instead of learning the techniques and strategies needed to deal with them, they give up.

In addition, people lack the consistent education and personal support needed to help them get from where they are to where they want to be. And to make matters worse, they don't have access to the mentors who will help them overcome the problems they're facing, inspire and motivate them when things get hard, and guide them when they don't know what to do next because it's not in the textbooks.

When I first came across Agile, I didn't know where to start either. And although I was reading the Agile books and attending Agile events that provided good information about how to do Scrum, Kanban, etc., what I was struggling to find was any information about how to transition organisations – who had been doing Waterfall for many years – to Agile. And because I was convinced that transitioning to Agile was in the best interest of the company I was with back then, in the absence of expert guidance I pushed and pushed and pushed for the change – until I eventually pushed myself out of a job. You see, that's one of the things about Agile transition: it's a very sensitive area. And even though your intentions are good and the change you are advocating might be in the best interest of your organisation, if that change is not positioned or managed correctly, it can quickly backfire.

At the point that this happened to me, I had to stop and ask myself why. Why wasn't I able to create change, even though that change had the potential to give the company a competitive advantage, significantly reduce their costs, and increase their profits? And in order to get the answer to that question I went in search of the world's top experts and leading authorities on behavioural and organisational change. Since then, I am fortunate to have been mentored by world renowned experts such as Tony Robbins (as you know, Tony Robbins is an expert in the area of personal change who works with Presidents, Prime Ministers, Royalty, Sport Champions, and people serious about achieving more in all areas of their lives), Brian Tracy (business and personal development expert),

# PREFACE

Kim and Robert Kiyosaki (author of the "Rich Dad, Poor Dad" wealth creation series), just to name a few. And aside from helping me understand where I went wrong in the past, they also taught me how to create behavioural and organisational change moving forward.

Wanting to get a better understanding of Agile and what it takes to successfully transition an organisation from Waterfall to Agile, I also went in search of the world's leading Agile experts and thought leaders. And since then, I've been fortunate to interview[1] – and be mentored by – top Agile experts such as Arie van Bennekum (Agile Manifesto author and DSDM pioneer), Jeff Sutherland (Agile Manifesto author and Scrum co-creator), Ron Jefferies (Agile Manifesto author and XP co-founder), Tom and Mary Poppendieck (originators of Lean Software Development), Jeff Patton, (User Story Mapping creator) and Esther Derby (world leader in Agile retrospectives), amongst others. And with the information, guidance, and support they gave, and continue to give, I have been able to create lasting, impactful change that has greatly benefitted me personally and the organisations I work with.

For example, once when I was moving from one job to another, my wages went up by £15,000. Imagine that: a £15,000 raise as a direct result of providing so much value in a previous role. Great, right? And another time, whilst working on a large multi-million pound project that was losing lots of money, I was given a contract extension at a time when 75% of the workforce was

---

[1] Available on www.AgileTV.co.uk

made redundant. The reason why I was given that extension was because even though I joined the project nearly two years in (when most of the damage had already been done), in the short time I was there I used Agile strategies and techniques to stop them losing even more, thereby saving them millions of pounds. You'll learn some of those techniques and strategies in this book. And even now, as I continue to work with some of the largest brands in regards to their Agile transition objectives, not only am I being given more authority and getting paid more, I'm also constantly getting head-hunted by companies who want to enlist my services.

So do you think that puts me in a place of security, even at a time when most people no longer have job security? Of course it does. And here's the thing about it: nothing I'm doing is rocket science because the truth is . . . there's nothing special about me. I'm just an average person who's driven to provide as much value as I can and help people like you to achieve similar results, because, with the right tools, information, and guidance, you can successfully introduce Agile practices into your organisation – and get paid more in the process.

Now, if you're like most people, at some time or other you might have wondered why some people succeed in life and others don't. This question intrigued me for many years and led me to extensive research and writing a book[2] on the key characteristics and traits of the world's most successful people.

---

[2] **Laugh Last, Laugh Loudest**: *How To Confidently Overcome Fear, Doubt and Criticism & Confidently Succeed In Business* (available from Amazon, Barnes and Noble and all good bookshops)

## PREFACE

And from studying the lives and achievements of household names such as Oprah Winfrey, Bill Gates, and the late Steve Jobs, plus spending time with successful entrepreneurs like Sir Richard Branson, Lord Alan Sugar, and Martha Lane Fox (lastminute.com co-founder), one of the things I discovered is that successful people are hungry, hungry in the sense that they know exactly what they want, and, come rain or shine, they are prepared to do whatever it takes (within the boundaries of their personal values) to get it. And they don't let the economy, other people, or circumstances stop them.

Another thing I discovered is that successful people go the extra mile. Think about it, most people do just enough work so they don't get fired, which is why companies pay them just enough money so that they keep coming back. And then people wonder why they have "more month at the end of the money" and struggle financially. Looking at the Olympics, we see that often the difference between winning and losing is a fraction of a second, which is why top performers push themselves to the limit. Driven by continuous improvement and a strong desire to be the best at what they do, successful people never stop learning. Instead, they stay up-to-date with the latest techniques and strategies relevant to their field because they recognise that is how to stay on top of their game and ahead of the competition. Successful people also adopt a long term perspective, planting seeds in the short term that will give them a bountiful harvest in the future.

Finally, and possibly most importantly, successful people actively seek out mentors. Looking at Presidents, Prime Ministers, world class footballers, champion golfers, Olympic gold medallists, Oscar winners, and the world's most successful business people, you'll see they all have advisors, trainers, coaches or mentors, etc., because they know that they can only get so far on their own. But when we tap (directly or indirectly) into the experience and knowledge of credible mentors, we achieve our goals easier and much faster.

This book enables you to tap into that experience and knowledge. Based on years of personal experience and the experience, knowledge, and wisdom of the world's leading experts in the areas of Agile software development, personal development, and organisational change, this book has been put together to serve as a practical guide to Agile transition. According to Pareto, 80% of what we need to know will come from 20% of what we actively learn. And recognising that people today lead busy lives and are struggling with information overload, I have distilled all the information collected over the years (at a considerable financial cost) into this easy to read book.

The proven techniques and strategies in this book are simple, effective, and relatively easy to use. And because they've been tried and tested many times, they're guaranteed to work for you if properly applied – because knowledge is power only when properly applied.

## PREFACE

I wish you great success in using this information to achieve all the things you want in your career and other areas of your life.

**Ade Shokoya**

*"That some achieve great success, is proof to all that others can achieve it as well."*
**Abraham Lincoln**

# PREFACE

CHAPTER 1

# Beware of the Lion That Inherited the Wrong Kingdom

*"The truth is incontrovertible. Malice may attack it, ignorance may deride it, but in the end, there it is. "*
**Winston Churchill**

The famous writer Mark Twain once said, *"It ain't what you don't know that gets you into trouble. It's what you know for sure that just ain't so."* In other words, what we <u>think</u> we know can sometimes keep us from knowing what we need to know. Let me demonstrate this by asking you a simple question:

What animal is king of the jungle?

Everyone knows the correct answer is "Lion", right? But there's a fundamental flaw with this answer. Do you know what it is? The fundamental flaw is . . .

Lions don't live in the jungle. They never have. Their natural habitat is, and has always been, the savannah and grassland.

And although they do occasionally venture into the bush or forest, most lions have never seen a jungle, let alone been in one. That's an example of how what we think we know can prevent us from knowing what we need to know.

So before we take a look at the techniques and strategies that will give you more influence in your organisation and greater control over your career, let's start by first dispelling a number of Agile myths because this will give you a solid foundation to build on.

**Myth 1 – Agile Is a Methodology**

Contrary to popular belief Agile is not a methodology. It is, however, an umbrella term used to collectively refer to a number of incremental processes and methodologies such as Scrum, Kanban, XP, DSDM, Behaviour Driven Design (BDD) and Test Driven Development (TDD). Although each methodology may adopt a different approach to software development, in reality there's not much difference between them because they're all value driven and able to respond quickly to change. Hence they are Agile.

In fact, Agile Manifesto author and XP co-creator Ron Jefferies once told me that upon reflection, he and the other manifesto authors wish they had done more in the early years of Agile to emphasise the similarities between the methodologies because today, too much focus is being placed on the differences instead of what they all have in common. Hopefully this will change with time.

## Myth 2 – Agile Methods Do Not Require Documentation

Another myth is that Agile projects are not supported by any documentation. This is commonly the result of a general misunderstanding of the Agile Manifesto value of *"Working software over comprehensive documentation."* But what people are missing is that the Agile Manifesto also states, *"While there is value in the items on the right, we value the items on the left more."*

Agile projects do require documentation, and the focus is on providing the right level of documentation at the right time so the development teams have exactly what they need when they need it in order to complete the tasks at hand. This "lightweight" approach eliminates the time and financial waste associated with creating "heavyweight" fifty page documents that most people won't even read.

## Myth 3 – Labelling It 'Agile' Makes It Agile

As Agile practices grow in popularity, more and more organisations are becoming aware of the benefits Agile has to offer. But rather than making the necessary organisational, cultural, and environmental changes required to achieve those benefits, many organisations are simply slapping "Agile" related labels on what they're already doing, thinking that makes them Agile. And when things don't turn out as expected, Agile gets the blame.

But just as calling a dog a cat doesn't make it so, re-labelling traditional software development methods "Agile" does not make them Agile. It takes more than that.

**Myth 4 – Agile Projects Are Not Planned**

Born out of the misunderstanding of another Agile Manifesto value, *"responding to change over following a plan,"* according to this myth, Agile projects are unplanned. This is far from the truth because successful Agile projects are planned, and unlike traditional projects where plans tend to be more rigid, recognising that things change, Agile plans are more flexible. As a result, Agile practices can be adapted to most projects and situations.

**Myth 5 – Agile is a 'Silver Bullet' Solution**

Because of the number of success stories that are a direct result of using Agile practices, many organisations are beginning to view Agile as the answer to all their project problems. Yes, Agile is a proven way of increasing quality, cutting costs, getting a quicker return on investment and gaining a competitive advantage. But it's just as likely to expose all the underlying cultural, political, operational and even 'people' related issues that might be the root cause of those problems.

Unfortunately, many organisations are not ready to even admit that they have those issues, let alone address them. This is why it's important to understand that Agile is not a silver bullet, because failing to do so could cost you dearly - like it has many others. If you sell Agile to your organisation or clients as the solution to all project woes, only for them to find out otherwise after they have committed the necessary time and resources, it could cost you your credibility and job in the long run – which I'm sure is something you wouldn't want to happen, would you? Therefore, be aware that although Agile has the potential to positively impact your software development process, it is not a silver bullet.

Now that we've dispelled some of the most common Agile myths, it's time for you to discover exactly how Agile can give you greater job security, quicker promotions, and increased income.

CHAPTER 2

# Beginning with the End in Mind

*"One day Alice came to a fork in the road and saw a Cheshire cat in a tree. "Which road do I take?" she asked. "Where do you want to go?" was his response. "I don't know," Alice answered. "Then," said the cat, "it doesn't matter."*
**Lewis Carroll, author**

In Stephen Covey's bestselling book, *The 7 Habits of Highly Effective People,* he talks about "beginning with the end in mind," a habit common amongst successful people from every walk of life. Take Bill Gates, for example: when he started Microsoft, he had a clear vision of a computer on every desk and in every home. And although at the time people doubted that dream could come true, that vision guided him to the present day where, not only did it come true, it also made him the richest person in the world for 13 years.

This demonstrates the fact that in order to increase the likelihood of success in any undertaking, it's important to first have a clear objective in mind. That's because objectives give us meaningful and measurable goals to work towards. They help us create a roadmap towards an end destination, work out a strategy of how to get there, and overcome the inevitable obstacles we're likely to face along the way.

Think about it: when you need to get home from somewhere, because you know what your objective and end destination is, you can work out how to get there. Whether you're walking or driving, you know what route to take. If you're catching a bus, train, or combination of both, you know which ones to take, including where you need to get on, where to change, and where to get off. And even if there are disruptions on your normal route, because you are working towards a clear objective of getting home, the chances are you will know or find alternative routes that will get you there.

The American football coach George Halas once said, *"Many people flounder about in life because they do not have a purpose, an objective toward which to work."* And because it's important that you have a clear objective in mind before transitioning to Agile, here are a few questions that might help you establish what that objective might be:

- Why are you considering Agile?
- What results do you expect to get from it?
- Are there any alternatives that can produce similar results for less effort?

The answers to those questions will help you identify whether Agile is right for you. For example, if you were considering implementing Agile because . . .

. . . you thought it was a silver bullet that would solve all your project problems, you now know it's not.

. . . everyone's talking about it and it seems to be the next "cool thing", you might want to take a moment to consider how well your existing methods are working. Because the truth is, for all the criticisms traditional methods get, there are instances of Waterfall projects that deliver on time, within budget, and to a high level of quality. If that holds true for you, it might be worth remembering the old saying, *"If it's not broke, don't fix it."* So if Waterfall is working for you, but there's room for improvement, which there always is, you might want to consider whether there is anything that can be done to make your existing processes better without transitioning to Agile.

. . . because you recognise Agile has the potential to reduce your time to market, increase your output quality, lower your costs, and give you quicker returns on investment, then you might want to keep on reading.

Aside from giving you direction, beginning with the end in mind will also help you define your strategy for getting there. For example, if your objective is to create better quality software, you might consider introducing pair programming or automated testing into your development process. Alternatively, if your goal is to reduce the bottlenecks in your existing delivery process, you might opt for an Agile flow system like Kanban.

Objectives are also important in helping us overcome obstacles. They motivate and give us a reason to continue in pursuit of our goals (our planned milestones) even when we do not feel like it. For example, if you have a job right now, the chances are you get paid. But the real reason you do what you do is not for the sake of having electronic or paper money, which has no intrinsic value. You cannot eat or wear it, but because of what that money does for you, your self-esteem, and your quality of life, e.g., pay your mortgage, provide for your family, invest for the future, etc., you welcome it. It is end goals like these that motivate us to get out of bed, get dressed, and go to work on those cold, wet, dark mornings when all we want to do is stay wrapped up in our warm beds.

Similarly, as you transition from Waterfall to Agile, it's your end vision that will help you overcome the obstacles and challenges you're sure to encounter along the way. So be sure to have a clear objective for your Agile transition.

And in the next chapter, you'll discover the most important thing you need to get started.

CHAPTER 3

# The Starting Point

*"Do what you can, with what you have, where you are."*
**Theodore Roosevelt**

One of my mentors, the international motivational speaker, Les Brown, often says: *"It's not what we don't have, it's what we think we need that keeps us from being successful or happy in life."* And there's great truth in that statement.

Think about it.

Most people wait for everything to be "just right" before they do the things that will make them happier in life. They wait for the "right time" to leave the job they've hated for many years or the right time to start the business they've dreamed about as far back as they can remember. They wait for: the right time to tell their nearest and dearest how much they really love them and, unfortunately, sometimes they're too late; the right time to leave an abusive marriage or relationship that has robbed them of their happiness for many, many years; and they wait for the right time to sort out their finances, even though debt might have been crippling them for many years. Then they wonder why nothing ever changes and they're unhappy in life.

But the irony is that the right conditions don't always present themselves; we have to create them. That's when things change for us. But if we wait for all the right conditions to present themselves before we do anything, we could be in for a very, very long wait.

Looking back, we see that some of the greatest advancements in the history of the human race have been initiated by proactive individuals who didn't wait for circumstances to be just right before taking action. Instead, they made the most of what they had, where they were. From Mahatma Gandhi to Winston Churchill, Abraham Lincoln to Nelson Mandela, Thomas Edison to Steve Jobs, we see what change agents can achieve against all odds. And today, you and I are still benefitting from their efforts.

When we wait for circumstances and other people to change before we take action to change the things we know we need to change, what we are really doing is giving away our personal power. And when we relinquish our personal power, our happiness, self-esteem, and wellbeing become dependent on external factors we have little or no control over. Then, like a rudderless ship, we end up going wherever the wind blows us.

However, by proactively taking steps, no matter how small, towards the things we want in life (be it a successful Agile transition, happier relationships, more rewarding jobs, improved financial situations, better health, etc.) we take control of our lives. That is why Mahatma Ghandi once said, *"Be the change you want to see in this world."*

If your organisation is new to Agile, chances are you will encounter a number of obstacles and constraints in regards to your Agile transition. Those constraints may range from the political environment you're operating in, through to a lack of understanding about Agile. They might also include infrastructural, logistical, and environmental constraints that don't support Agile practices. When faced with all these challenges it's tempting to wait for things to be *just right* before embarking on your Agile transition.

However, there's a reason why you are reading this book right now, which is likely to be because you see the potential benefits Agile practices have to offer you and your organisation. And because that makes you a visionary, it's important you do not fall victim to procrastination. Instead, start where you are and do the best with what you've got. Because, as an Agile change agent, part of your role will be to unearth and (where possible) remove any constraints, be they political, cultural, operational, or logistical, that might be impeding your organisation's Agile transition. Doing so will increase your long-term chances of success, so don't wait for the conditions to be just right. Start where you are and do your best with what you've got.

Now let's be honest: changing things isn't always easy, especially when you don't know what steps to take to make that change happen. So in the next chapter you will find an overview that will help you get started with your Agile transition, with more detailed steps covered in each of the subsequent chapters.

CHAPTER 4

# If You Don't Know This Then Your Agile Transition Is Likely to Fail

*"What do you want to achieve or avoid? The answers to this question are objectives. How will you go about achieving your desired results? The answer to this you can call strategy."*
**William E Rothschild**

When considering a transition from traditional Waterfall development to Agile practices, it's important to be aware that the organisation's existing size and culture will have a big impact on the strategy you might want to use.

For example, if you work for a large or small organisation with less rigid processes, that is not bogged down by too much internal politics and welcomes change, then you might want to use a transformation strategy. On the other hand, if you are a part of an organisation, large or small, with very rigid processes, that is plagued by lots of internal politics and is slow to change, then you might be better off using an adoption strategy.

And here's the difference between the two: Agile transformation strategies are value driven. They focus on changing organisational culture; the way people work, interact, and communicate, based on the Agile Manifesto values and principles. And because transformation strategies place greater value on *"individuals and interactions over processes and tools,"* there tends to be more emphasis on developing and empowering people so that they can be more productive. Because they adopt a long-term perspective, Agile transformation strategies tend to produce longer lasting results. So, although it might take more time and effort to transform a company, considering that people are an organisation's biggest asset, it's easy to see why some of the world's most successful companies invest so heavily in them.

That said, there are many organisations that have built their existence (and success) around heavily structured processes. And to ensure the business continues to do what it does, they invest the majority of their time and money into systems and tools. These are the organisations best suited to Agile adoption. Because adoption strategies are more process driven, they tend to focus on the implementation of specific Agile methodologies and creating structure by standardising them across the company.

Regardless of which one you choose, your transition strategy is likely to go through the following three stages:

**Understand:** Before we can create meaningful change in anything, it's important to first understand what it is that we are trying to change. We need to know where the organisation is now and where it wants to be in the future, the business objectives, organisational culture, political environment, etc. Understanding leads to clarity, and with clarity it becomes easier to identify what needs to be changed.

**Educate:** People are habitual and tend to be most comfortable doing what they already know. So if you want people to do something different (especially something they may not have any prior experience in, or knowledge of) it's important to first educate them as to why they should do things differently. It's also just as important, if not more so, for you to maintain your own education and ensure your relevant skillset is up to date.

**Execute:** Change is created through action. So once you have understood what needs to be changed and educated people on why and how to make that change, then you need to take action towards creating that change.

Note that execution does not end the cycle. In fact, it gives birth to another one. Because when we act on what we know, we often learn more; and the more we understand, the better positioned we are to educate others based on our newfound knowledge. And knowing more enables us to do more.

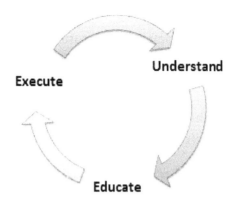

**Figure 1:** Understand, Educate & Execute Cycle

Depending on the size and culture of your organisation, here are a few ideas[3] on which strategies might be best suited to you:

**Large Organisation, Less Rigid Processes and Low Political Environment**

This type of organisation may have ad-hoc or home grown processes which could be a symptom of fast growth. Although the lack of processes and/or politics might make it easier to experiment with Agile, you may run into challenges if the culture is one where no natural conflict occurs and everyone maintains the status quo.

---

[3] Adapted from session hand-outs provided by Jason Little at Agile 2011

**Understand:**

- Why is the company structured the way it is; e.g., is it a home-grown company that has been unable to define processes due to fast growth?
- What obvious strengths and weaknesses does the existing structure create?
- What end results are expected from Agile?
- Based on the Schneider Model, what is the organisation's existing cultural type and what potential issues might it be covering up?

**Educate:**

- Learn about Lean Software Development and identifying waste.
- Join local Agile groups to gain insights from peers or Agile coaches/consultants.
- Introduce the organisation to Agile through informal methods; e.g., wikis, study groups, workshops, etc., before getting started.

**Execute**

- Get feedback from colleagues and a feel for the organisational mood towards Agile.
- Create a pilot team.

- Focus less on the processes/methodologies and more on Agile's adaptability to different situations.

**Small Organisation, Less Rigid Processes and Low Political Environment**

Employees in this type of organisation tend to have stronger and healthier relationships compared with larger or more rigid ones. Therefore, depending on the existing culture, they are more likely to be receptive to Agile values and principles. This is an ideal environment for trying stuff out fast and early.

**Understand:**
- What does your organisation expect to achieve from Agile?
- How do Agile values and principles map to the existing organisational culture?
- What work is done?

**Educate:**
- Learn the basics of the main Agile methodologies.
- Start study groups and discuss Agile related topics; e.g., blog posts, articles, books, webinars.
- Join local Agile user groups and arrange to host a local event at your office, if possible.

**Execute:**

- Based on your understanding of what work is done and what outcomes are expected, experiment with different Agile processes to see which is best suited.

## Large Organisation, More Rigid Processes and Highly Political Environment

The political environment within this type of organisation might make it hard to create cross-functional teams consisting of people from different departments. In addition, if your organisation is big on processes, then the Agile values and principles might conflict with the existing culture.

**Understand:**

- The political landscape and the extent of your sphere of influence.
- Where is the support for Agile?
- Depending on the size of the organisation, your Agile transition is likely to be slow – and sometimes painful.

**Educate:**

- Learn about the differences between strategic and tactical Agile.
- Join local Agile groups to gain insights from peers or Agile coaches/consultants.

- Subscribe to online Agile expert webinars; e.g., VersionOne, Sticky Minds.

**Execute:**

- Focus on your sphere of influence, including those already in support of Agile.

- Take small steps because too much change too quickly may have an adverse effect.

- Beware of *"mandated Agile"*.

## Small Organisation, More Rigid Processes and Highly Political Environment

The political environment within this type of organisation might make it hard to create cross-functional teams consisting of people from different departments. In addition, if your organisation is big on processes then the Agile values and principles might conflict with the existing culture.

**Understand:**

- What's driving the rigid process?

- Who stands to gain or lose from an Agile transition?

- What are the business objectives and which Agile practices can help achieve them?

**Educate:**

- Take a closer look at Lean & Kanban processes; they require less change.
- Join local Agile groups to gain insights from peers or Agile coaches/consultants.

**Execute:**

- Where possible, avoid using the "A" word as it might create conflict and resistance based on a misconception that Agile is chaotic.
- Make existing work and processes visible.
- Introduce measuring metrics and collect data.

Whatever strategy you decide to go for, always keep in mind these words from Winston Churchill: *"However beautiful the strategy, you should occasionally look at the results."*

# The Secret Ninja Weapon That Leads to Organisational Change

*"It's easier to ask for forgiveness than permission"*
**U.S. Navy Rear Admiral Grace Hopper**

Growing up, I was a big fan of Kung Fu movies. I loved watching Bruce Lee, Jackie Chan, and the *Karate Kid* (I still remember spending hours balancing on one leg trying to perfect that Karate Kid move). I also loved watching the Ninjas.

As you know, the Ninjas were an elite fighting force whose origins can be traced back to early feudal Japan. Mainly used for assassination and spying missions, one of their most effective weapons was the element of surprise. Masters of stealth, the Ninja would appear out of nowhere, complete their mission, and then disappear again, adding to the mystery and intrigue surrounding them.

Stealth is also a powerful weapon available to you in the form of something called "Stealth Agile". Usually done "below the radar," Stealth Agile can be an effective way to bypass bureaucracy when introducing Agile into an organisation. An approach typically favoured by those at the lower end of an organisation's hierarchy, Agile practices are applied to a pilot or existing project with the objective of generating results that are then used to present a case to key decision makers as to why Agile might be a viable option. Here's an example of how it works in practice:

A few years ago, I was called in to work on a high profile project for one of the UK's largest outsourcing companies. The project had been going for just over two years when I joined and the teams were geographically dispersed between the UK and India. After being on the project for nearly six months and seeing it was running behind schedule and over budget, it became apparent that Kanban (an Agile flow process) might be a viable solution. So I spoke to my line manager to get her thoughts and a feel for what the political environment was like and how receptive the organisation was to change. She explained to me that at the beginning of the project one of the teams implemented Kanban with disastrous results and as a result, Kanban was now considered to be a "swear" word within the organisation, especially at senior management level.

Still convinced that a properly implemented Kanban system would solve some of the project issues, I informed my line manager that I would be experimenting with the methodology in my small team – and within a few weeks of adopting Kanban we became the most efficient team on the project. We were developing features quicker, raising fewer bugs, and having

CHAPTER 5

# The Secret Ninja Weapon That Leads to Organisational Change

*"It's easier to ask for forgiveness than permission"*
**U.S. Navy Rear Admiral Grace Hopper**

Growing up, I was a big fan of Kung Fu movies. I loved watching Bruce Lee, Jackie Chan, and the *Karate Kid* (I still remember spending hours balancing on one leg trying to perfect that Karate Kid move). I also loved watching the Ninjas.

As you know, the Ninjas were an elite fighting force whose origins can be traced back to early feudal Japan. Mainly used for assassination and spying missions, one of their most effective weapons was the element of surprise. Masters of stealth, the Ninja would appear out of nowhere, complete their mission, and then disappear again, adding to the mystery and intrigue surrounding them.

Stealth is also a powerful weapon available to you in the form of something called "Stealth Agile". Usually done "below the radar," Stealth Agile can be an effective way to bypass bureaucracy when introducing Agile into an organisation. An approach typically favoured by those at the lower end of an organisation's hierarchy, Agile practices are applied to a pilot or existing project with the objective of generating results that are then used to present a case to key decision makers as to why Agile might be a viable option. Here's an example of how it works in practice:

A few years ago, I was called in to work on a high profile project for one of the UK's largest outsourcing companies. The project had been going for just over two years when I joined and the teams were geographically dispersed between the UK and India. After being on the project for nearly six months and seeing it was running behind schedule and over budget, it became apparent that Kanban (an Agile flow process) might be a viable solution. So I spoke to my line manager to get her thoughts and a feel for what the political environment was like and how receptive the organisation was to change. She explained to me that at the beginning of the project one of the teams implemented Kanban with disastrous results and as a result, Kanban was now considered to be a "swear" word within the organisation, especially at senior management level.

Still convinced that a properly implemented Kanban system would solve some of the project issues, I informed my line manager that I would be experimenting with the methodology in my small team – and within a few weeks of adopting Kanban we became the most efficient team on the project. We were developing features quicker, raising fewer bugs, and having fewer issues. All this did not go unnoticed by our product owner and colleagues. And because everyone wanted to know how we were getting the results we were getting, my line manager asked me to deliver a presentation.

In the presentation, I highlighted some of the problems my team faced before we started using Kanban. These were common problems across the teams, so everybody could relate to them. Then I proceeded to show them what changes we had made and how those changes had impacted our results. Needless to say, the presentation was well received, and the attendees went and told their line managers that they needed to see what we were doing.

Around that time, in an attempt to reduce the amount of money the project was losing, around 75% of the project team had their contracts terminated early . . . myself included. However, the line managers still wanted to see the results of my pilot project, so I delivered another presentation which they told senior management about. This resulted in me having to deliver yet another presentation, this time to senior management and, at the end of which, they unanimously agreed to roll Kanban out across the whole project. The following day I was offered a contract extension and asked to lead the rollout across the UK and Indian teams.

Now here's the thing: based on the nature of the project and the problems it was facing, I felt Kanban would be a better fit before I started a pilot project. But being aware of the political environment and senior management's negative views of

Kanban at the time, I realised that presenting verbal reasons for transitioning to Kanban would fall on deaf ears. Instead, I used Stealth Agile to create a buzz and visible results that led to the decision makers reaching that conclusion themselves.

Now, the reason I'm sharing this with you is not to impress you, but rather to impress upon you how effective Stealth Agile is as a transitional strategy (it also demonstrates how Agile can give you greater job security). Based on the belief that, *"It's easier to ask for forgiveness than permission,"* Stealth Agile is an effective tool for avoiding bureaucracy and bypassing resistance to Agile. Executing Stealth Agile with a small team or pilot project enables you to try something different under controlled and manageable conditions . . . so if things do not work out quite as planned, it's unlikely there will be much to be "forgiven" for.[4]

Success with Stealth Agile hinges on two key factors, which you will discover in the following chapters.

---

[4] Now, of course, some organisations are so political they might not be "forgiving" of people trying something new. And if your organisation is like that, you might want to consider whether you really want to work in a place that penalises people for showing personal initiative and trying to create a competitive advantage.

CHAPTER 6

# How to Eat an Elephant

*"Victory is won not in miles but in inches. Win a little now, hold your ground, and later, win a little more."*
**Louis L'Amour**

Q**uestion:** How do you eat an elephant?

The only way to eat an elephant is bit-by-bit, by taking small bite-sized chunks. But in life, many people try to eat the whole elephant in one sitting by going for all or nothing. However, what they fail to realise is that going for all or nothing often results in nothing.

In some way, this is the mentality the Waterfall approach to software development is based on because it assumes a perfect and complete understanding of everything that needs to be known about the system before development begins, including costs, timeframe, how it will be used, etc. It also assumes that each of the development phases will go according to plan, and that a fully functional system will be ready to hand over to a satisfied customer after testing.

But as you and I already know, things rarely go that smoothly in reality because the testing phase usually uncovers bugs that result in us having to go back through each of the previous phases to find and fix the root cause. And assuming we do get the system to function as expected, by the time we deliver it to the customer there's always the possibility that their requirements will have changed. Or worse: we discover that because the requirements were miscommunicated or misunderstood, we have perfectly developed the wrong thing. Ouch!

With Agile projects, this issue is addressed by using an incremental approach where small pieces of value are developed and delivered to the customer on a regular basis. Focused on taking small steps towards achieving the bigger goal, the objective is to create quick wins.

Quick wins are also important to your success with Stealth Agile, because results speak louder than words – especially when trying to convince people to do things differently. That's not to say there's no value in verbally communicating the benefits of Agile practices, but talking can get you only so far. However, when people can clearly see how doing things differently will benefit them, they are more likely to engage in the required change. And the best way to convince your organisation that transitioning to Agile is in their best interest is to prove it with results.

Proven results add to your credibility. And since people are more likely to follow recommendations that come from credible sources, being credible makes it easier for you to secure the support of senior management and key decision makers within your organisation, thereby increasing your sphere of influence. That's why it's important to achieve quick wins, because they give you tangible, measurable results to put forward when presenting your case in favour of Agile. And the great thing is, when your proposition is supported by visible results, you don't have to go for a "hard sell". Instead, you simply present the facts, clearly demonstrating what the problem was before you started using Agile practices, and the results you achieved on your pilot project after applying it. And assuming there's a significant difference between your "before" and "after" situation, a decision to implement Agile – even if it's just on an "official" pilot project – should be a no-brainer.

This brings us neatly on to the second factor important to your success with Stealth Agile.

CHAPTER 7

# Doing This Will Help You Stand Out

*"Seeing is believing."*
**American Proverb**

As a youngster, I got many hours of pleasure from reading superhero stories in the Marvel comic series. And back then one of my favourite superheroes was the Invisible Girl from the Fantastic Four.

Why?

Because as a young, inquisitive child full of energy, I always seemed to be getting into trouble . . . obviously through no fault of my own. And the times when I had supposedly "broken" my mother's vase (technically it wasn't me; it was the ball that bounced off my foot), or a neighbours window (what can I say; the ball had it in for me), I really wished I had the power to become invisible, too.

Being invisible is great when you're doing things you don't want anyone to see or know about. But when you're building trust and credibility using the Stealth Agile strategy, it's important to be transparent and highly visible. Because the reality is, we all want to achieve more for ourselves. So when people see you're getting noticeably better results than they are in the same area, they're likely to become inquisitive, wanting to know what you're doing different and how they can get the same results too.

You see, most people are suspicious of new things, especially those they don't understand. So the more secretive you are about what you're doing, the more suspicious and resistant to your proposed change they will become. However, by being transparent you give people less to be suspicious about, thereby making it easier to build trust. Another reason for making your progress visible is that it enables you to showcase your "quick wins". And you know, quick wins are essential for building credibility and securing the support of key decision makers.

One way to achieve transparency on Agile projects is by using "information radiators". An information radiator is defined by Agile Manifesto author, Alistair Cockburn, as *"a display posted in a place where people can see it as they work or walk by. It shows readers information they care about without having to ask anyone a question. This means more communication with fewer interruptions."* [5]

---

[5] Crystal Clear: A Human-Powered Methodology for Small Teams (Alistair Cockburn)

Often referred to as "Scrum Boards" (in Scrum) or "Kanban Boards" (in Kanban), information radiators are an effective way of communicating project status, issues, or key project metrics with minimum effort, thereby making critical project information visible and easily accessible to all. Information radiators can also be a catalyst for organisational change. For example, whilst recently having a meal with a senior manager of one of the largest companies in the United States, he shared the following experience that clearly demonstrates just how effective visibility and transparency can be for creating organisational change.

When his IT department first started using the popular Agile methodology, Scrum, they put a Scrum board up on a wall to ensure everyone had visibility of the relevant project information. A few months later, whilst walking past the accounting department he noticed that they had something on their wall that looked similar to the Scrum board on the wall of his IT department. So he stepped in for a closer look. He was then approached by a lady from the accounts department who asked him what he was doing there. He explained that he was from the IT department and whilst passing he noticed the Scrum board on the wall and out of interest, wanted to take a closer look. The lady from accounts then said that her department had not realised it was called a Scrum board and went on to explain that a few months earlier, one of her team members had been down in the IT department when he saw the board on the wall. Thinking it would be a great way of managing their workflows in the accounts department, he told the rest of the team about the board, and after a few other team members had been down to IT to check it out, the accounting department created their own one, even though they did not know what it was called at the time. She then went on to ask the IT manager if he could find some time to help them get a better understanding of how to use the board more effectively.

What this example clearly demonstrates is the positive psychological impact that transparency and quick wins can have when it comes to creating behavioural change. You see, because we don't like being manipulated or forced into doing things, people are more likely to resist any change they feel is being imposed on them. And because we like to make our own decisions, or at least feel like we have, at a subconscious level we tend to be suspicious of anyone we think is trying to force change on us. But when we feel like the decision to change is our own, we are more likely to engage in that change, especially if we're able to see the potential benefits that change will bring us.

So with that in mind, make sure your results and quick wins are visible for all to see. And in the next chapter you will discover what you can do to significantly increase your chances of success with your Agile transition.

CHAPTER 8

# How to Influence People by Tuning into the World's Favourite Radio Station

*"You can have everything in life you want, if you will just help other people get what they want."*
**Zig Ziglar**

Most people are familiar with the fact that sun rays focused through a magnifying glass on a single spot will burn a hole in a piece of paper. The sun is a big ball of energy capable of destroying anything that gets too close. But by the time its electromagnetic waves reach the earth, that energy is so dispersed that without the magnifying glass, the sun would only warm the paper. Similarly, lasers are concentrated beams of light so powerful that they can cut through most materials, including metals.

What this tells us is that focused energy has greater impact. And instead of trying to change your organisation on your own, you are likely to have greater success by concentrating your time and energy on the key people within your sphere of influence, especially since Stealth Agile conducted in isolation will only get you so far.

In the story I shared in a previous chapter, about the time I used Stealth Agile to transition a large, geographically dispersed organisation to Kanban, you will note that before starting, I secured my line manager's support by informing her that I would be experimenting with Kanban. As a result, in the early stages, she was very influential in raising the profile of what my team was doing. In fact, she was the one who arranged the first presentation.

In Malcolm Gladwell's bestselling book, *Tipping Point: How Little Things Can Make a Big Difference,* he identifies the following three types of people who are key to making change in any area (political, social, organisational, etc.):

**Mavens** – "information specialists"; people who expose others to new ideas and information.

**Connectors** – highly sociable people who spread new ideas and tend to have networks that span different social circles.

**Salesmen** – "persuaders"; charismatic people who have the ability to sway doubters over to new ideas.

According to Gladwell, this highly influential group of individuals are behind every form of major change, which is why it is highly recommended that you focus on getting their support because they are key to the success of your Agile transition. And if you don't already know who these people are within your organisation, here are a few questions that might help you identify them:

- Who are the key people within your immediate sphere of influence?
- Is their sphere of influence larger than yours?
- Are they forward thinkers or maintainers of the status quo?
- Are they likely to help or hinder your Agile transition?

Once you've identified who these key people are, it is important to be aware that, like most people, they will be tuned into the world's most popular radio station, WII-FM (What's In It For Me). That's the question running through their heads, and the one you will need to answer if you want to secure their support. And the way to help them answer that question is by demonstrating how transitioning to Agile is in their best interest. Show them how it will benefit them, make their job easier, help them hit their targets, get greater job satisfaction, etc.

The truth is that people prefer to stick within their comfort zone and continue doing things the way they always have done rather than to do things differently. That's because change requires effort and can be very uncomfortable, especially if there's a steep learning curve associated with it. So without compelling reasons for trading-in comfort for discomfort, most people won't – which is why it's important to give people strong reasons for supporting your Agile transition.

Be aware that reasons are likely to differ, depending on the person and what their position is. So in the next two chapters we'll be looking at some effective communication and persuasion techniques that will significantly increase your chances of securing the support you need.

CHAPTER 9

# Six Sure-Fire Ways to Get People to Agree with You

*"Persuasion is often more effectual than force."*
**Aesop**

If you've ever tried persuading someone to do something, you'll know just how hard it can be, especially if you and the other person don't know each other. Persuasion is a conscious attempt to influence other people's opinions or behaviours, and one of the keys to effective persuasion is rapport . . . because as a rule of thumb, *"people like each other like each other."*

One way to quickly build rapport is to see things from the other person's perspective, because doing so makes it easier for you to find something about their view that you can agree with, or at least appreciate. And as you already know, we all like being appreciated and agreed with, which is why very few arguments ever stem from matters of agreement (except for that dreaded question: "My bum looks big in this, doesn't it?" – but for obvious reasons, we won't go there).

Agreement is essential for building rapport, because agreement lowers defence. On the other hand, disagreement is often seen as a personal attack, causing people to become defensive and argue their position in an attempt to protect their egos. And once the ego kicks in, regardless of what factual information you put forward, the other person is likely to take an even stronger stance on their original position. That's why telling people they're wrong is a recipe for disaster. It arouses opposition and makes the listener want to engage in battle with you before you even start. But once you align yourself in agreement with others, it's easier to guide them, in a non-threatening way, towards a desired outcome.

An effective way of creating agreement in potentially volatile situations is to use the "Six Thinking Hats" approach. Created by Edward de Bono, a renowned writer regarded by many to be the leading authority in the field of creative and lateral thinking, the Six Thinking Hats is a simple yet effective parallel thinking process for directing groups or individuals towards a specific goal. The hats are metaphors for six distinct brain states represented by the following colours:

**White** – focused on information and facts known or needed

**Black** – cautious; devil's advocate focused on why something might not work

**Green** – focused on creativity and innovation

**Yellow** – positive, optimistic and focused on possibilities

**Red** – emotions; signifies feelings, hunches, and intuition

**Blue** – focused on structure, order, and processes

Now, it's important to be aware that what these hats do not represent is behaviour, but rather people's predominate way of thinking and approaching information. And although typically used to reach consensus in group decision making processes, the Six Thinking Hats can also be used to align with an individual's primary way of thinking, thereby making it easier to gain their support.

For example, if you want somebody with predominately white hat thinking to support your Agile transition, you might approach them with facts and figures along the following lines:

*"Considering that 44% of projects don't deliver the required functionality, 26% are cancelled or never used, and 60% to 80% of development cost is associated with development rework, there seems to be substantial opportunity for improvement.[6] And since a recent survey found that 87% of companies using Agile processes reported a significant improvement in their ability to respond to markets and requirements, 70% reported a significant improved time to market and quicker return on investment, and some companies reported revenue growth in the region of 8%, maybe it would be worth seeing if we can benefit from similar results, too."[7]*

Or, if you're talking to a predominately black hat thinker, you might start by highlighting that one of the challenges with Agile is it can be hard to establish total projects costs upfront, or that the benefits of Agile will not be visible overnight. This

---

[6] TechWell with IBM webinar
[7] State of Agile Development Survey 2010 by VersionOne

approach will align you with the black hat's critical mode of thinking, and then you can counter it with white hat thinking such as this:

*"However, the fact is that the cost and resources estimated at the beginning of Waterfall projects are very rarely accurate anyway, which is why so many projects tend to run over budget and much longer than scheduled. In fact, recent research from Oxford University looked at over 1,500 IT projects across the world and some of the key findings included: the planned costs of a project that overruns can end up being 200% of the original cost on average, and the IT sector is almost 3 times more likely to suffer from over-budget projects than the comparable construction sector.[8] So maybe not having all the costs upfront is not a bad thing after all because it will stop us falling into a false sense of security and forces us to keep a tighter rein on our on-going costs."*

If you're speaking to somebody with predominately green hat thinking, you might focus on how the iterative Agile approach will result in faster feedback and valuable information that can be used to improve quality, innovate and create better solutions, features, and products. Or if the person is a yellow hat thinker, you could focus on all the positive aspects of Agile including lower development costs, earlier return on investment, better quality, ability to respond quickly to changing economic and market conditions, etc. For red hat

---

[8] Innovative IT (http://www.innovativeit.co/news/IT-Projects-Likely-To-Run-Over-Budget/16)

thinkers you would focus on how Agile practices make work more rewarding by motivating and empowering individuals to self-organise. And finally, for blue hat thinkers you could focus on how Agile would give them greater visibility over the development process, enabling them to identify and respond to problems much earlier.

You can also use the Six Thinking Hats to align your presentations with the different thinking modes of the people in your audience, because by doing so you are likely to get a much higher level of agreement and consensus. The reason the Six Thinking Hats is such an effective persuasion tool is because it's based on the fact that people are most likely to be influenced by people who share similar views. By aligning yourself to another person's way of thinking, at a subconscious level you're communicating that you think like them too, thereby establishing common ground upon which to build further agreement.

So the next time you're trying to persuade someone to do something, remember to put your thinking cap on, but be careful not to make the embarrassing mistake I made, which I will share with you in the following chapter.

# The Thing That Motivates All Human Behaviour - and How to Use It to Your Advantage

*"The aim of the wise is not to secure pleasure, but to avoid pain."*
**Aristotle**

Around the age of 21, my girlfriend at the time (for the purpose of this story we'll call her "Lisa") and I decided to go away for a romantic weekend in Paris. We were both very excited because that was our first trip abroad together and we had planned all the things we were going to do once we got there.

On the day we were leaving, I arrived at Lisa's home and called the house phone to let her know I was outside. As soon as I heard the voice on the other end of the phone say, "Hello," I went on to tell her I was outside and cheekily asked if she had remembered to pack the "toys" we had bought for our "weekend" away. There was a short silence, and you can imagine my embarrassment when I heard the following words down the phone: "Hello, Ade. This is Lisa's mum speaking. I'll let her know you're outside. Goodbye." And then she hung up.

You see, what I had not realised up until that point was that Lisa and her mum sounded alike on the phone. And because I had not confirmed whom I was speaking to before opening my mouth, I ended up having one of those embarrassing conversations you don't want to have with your partner's mother.

It was then that I learnt the importance of knowing whom you're talking to before opening your mouth; this holds just as true when having private phone conversations as it does when trying to get support for your Agile transition.

As we established in a previous chapter, change is scary for people because it takes them out of their comfort zone into unknown territory where their status and expertise are under potential threat. And since most people are tuned into WII-FM radio (What's In It For Me?), it's a good idea, when proposing change, to show how that change aligns with their personal goals. This is why it's important to know what motivates the person we are talking to.

According to psychologists, all human behaviour is motivated by two fundamental factors: pain and pleasure. But what they also found was that people are more determined to move away from pain than they are to move towards pleasure. So, for that reason, when trying to gain support for your Agile transition it's a good idea to start by first emphasising people's current pain points and then demonstrating how Agile can help heal them.

For example, if you're speaking to a project manager who's having problems with a project that's running late and over budget, you could engage them in a dialogue along the following lines:

*"I've just come across something that might prevent future projects running over budget and time, and I was wondering if that would be off interest to you?"* If they are having these problems, the chances are they will be interested, at which point you could continue with: *"I appreciate that even with the best project plans in place it can still be hard and even frustrating managing changing requirements, unforeseen risks, and unrealistic delivery expectations. And I can see how those issues might create stress when there's little or no room to deviate from the original project plan, especially if the business/customer won't compromise on quality, cost, or time. That said, I am currently looking at something that many project managers, some of whom were previously in similar or worse situations than yours, are saying helped them turn their projects around and quickly identify, isolate, and resolve risks before they impacted their projects. It helped them have better visibility of project progress, thus making it easier to keep track of resources, cost, and time. And it helped them manage constantly changing requirements without having to worry about going over budget. Would you like to know more?"*

If you present something along these lines to project managers who can relate to these pain points, do you think they might want to know more? Off course they would, at which point you can proceed to explain or demonstrate exactly how Agile can help them resolve their problems.

Similarly, if you were talking to a developer who is unhappy with being micro-managed and had constantly changing requirements impacting their work, you could say:

*"I understand that someone constantly asking you for regular status updates and working with frequently changing requirements can lead to feelings of uncertainty, frustration, and even zap the fun out of doing what you do. But if there was a solution that ensured you always knew exactly what you would be working on over 2-4 week periods, that empowered you to personally choose the tasks you want to work on, freed you from micro-management, and put the fun back into your work, would you want to know more about it?"*

Obviously the above are just examples of things you might say, and it's important that you use words you're personally comfortable with. But the bottom line is, regardless of who you're trying to sell Agile to, it's important you:

1. Get to know who you are talking to.
2. Understand what their current problems and pain points are.
3. Demonstrate how Agile can help them solve those problems and achieve their desired outcomes.

That said, do bear in mind that sometimes people's perception of the pain associated with change can be greater than the pain they already associate with their current situation, which explains why some people stay in relationships that are clearly making them unhappy. So in the next chapter we'll be looking at what it takes to get people to take immediate action instead of putting things off till later.

CHAPTER 11

# Without This All Your Hard Work Will Come to Nothing

*"Without a sense of urgency, desire loses its value."*
**Jim Rohn**

Have you ever had one of those heart-to-heart conversations with a distressed friend or family member that ended with them stating what they were going to do differently in order to move beyond the situation causing their unhappiness; e.g., abusive relationship, serious financial problems, long term unemployment, etc? You leave feeling hopeful and happy for them, right? But that happiness quickly turns into frustration when next you see them and nothing has changed other than the fact that their situation has gotten even worse. At that point you might wonder why, with all the pain and unhappiness their current situation is causing them, they won't make the necessary changes that will help put their life back on track.

As you know, change requires effort and can be uncomfortable. And because people are creatures of habit, when comparing the pain and comfort of their current situation with the perceived pain and discomfort associated with change, some people opt for the "devil they know". However, if their current pain or the perceived future pain associated with doing nothing now is worse than the pain they associate with change, then they're likely to opt for the lesser of two evils.

Consider for a moment how people typically behave in the following situations:

> **Fire Alarm** – when a fire alarm goes off, if there are no obvious signs of immediate danger, people often watch to see how other people respond before taking any action.
>
> **Visible Smoke** – when there is smoke but no visible fire, people will typically start making their way to the nearest exit, still unsure of the extent of the emergency but taking preventive action just in case things turn out to be serious.
>
> **Visible Fire** – a visible fire creates a heightened sense of emergency which causes people to run out of a building in an attempt to avoid a potentially life-threatening situation.
>
> **Explosion** – explosions typically result in all hell breaking loose as people instantly sprint, push, jump, and do whatever it takes to get out of the building and escape the immediate threat to their life and wellbeing.

What this demonstrates is that people respond to situations differently depending on how much urgency they associate with their current situation, which is why establishing a sense of urgency is necessary to gain the cooperation required to drive a significant change effort.

Now, I'm not suggesting that you blow up your offices in order to create that sense of urgency. But you might want to consider the fact that purely intellectual based arguments, even those backed by solid business cases, are less likely to create urgency because they speak to the head, not the heart. However, when you "aim for the heart" and connect with people's personal values, your case for change will come alive, engage their senses, and inspire them to take action.

So following on from the project manager example in the previous chapter and assuming you've explained or demonstrated exactly how Agile will benefit them, you could create urgency by adding something along these lines:

*"Now, of course, we could leave our projects to continue as they are. But I'm sure you would agree that losing money in today's financially turbulent times could prove disastrous. And at a time like this when everyone is fighting to stay in business, the last thing we want to do is lose customers due to poor quality and overrun projects or because our competitors are able to deliver higher quality software faster and cheaper than us. That said, right now there's a unique opportunity for visionary leaders to take advantage of changes in the market and economy. And by making a few adjustments to how we currently do things, not only are we likely to increase our chances of survival during uncertain times, we also have the potential to increase our market share and create loyal customers by providing them with more value for their money. Doing so is not just in the company's best interest, it's also in our personal interests*

*because if the company is doing well, then there's less chance of us being made redundant."*

Once again, the above wording is just an example. The key is to tailor what you are saying to your audience so that it touches on their pain and pleasure points in a way you are comfortable with.

Now, before closing this chapter, let's be clear on something of great importance. As you can see, effective communication techniques are powerful tools for influencing people in all areas of life. So when you're using 'pain points' to influence people, make sure that pain is real because:

1. If it's real, the person will be able to relate to it because they have experienced it, are experiencing it, or are aware that it is a realistic potential future pain point.
2. Most importantly, creating fake pain points just to get people to do what you want is manipulation, lacks integrity, and is immoral.

The same holds true when you are conveying the potential pleasure points/benefits. They have to be real and hype free; no dangling of carrots you know you have no hope of delivering on.

So that's the caveat: **these effective communication techniques are only to be used in win-win situations, NEVER for the purpose of manipulation.**

In the next chapter, you'll learn how to avoid a common mistake that typically causes people to switch off and not hear what you have to say.

# How to Avoid a Common Mistake That's Sure to Leave Your Agile Transition Dead in the Water

*"Everyone hears only what he understands."*
**Johann Wolfgang von Goethe**

In my spare time, I work voluntarily mentoring young people from all backgrounds. It's something I've been doing for over 15 years now, and although sometimes it can be quite challenging, helping young people turn their lives around and achieve their goals is very rewarding.

Now, even though I have been doing this for so many years, one thing I still find very interesting is that regardless of their background, young people seem to have their own 'slang' that often makes little or no sense to older people. For example, if you heard a young person say, "That car is sick!" you would be forgiven for wondering why they are attributing feelings to an inanimate object. But what they're actually communicating is the car is really nice.

Confusing?

I agree. And that's something worth considering when speaking to people about Agile. Because if you use Agile jargon like, "WIP", "Scrumban", "daily stand ups", "sprints", etc., to explain the Agile software development process to people with no previous exposure to Agile practices, the chances are they will be confused too.

This is a mistake I used to make when I first started out in Agile many years ago. Back then I struggled to get management or clients to adopt Agile practices, even when it was obvious to all that traditional methods weren't working. Initially, that lead me to think the decision-makers were incompetent . . . at best. But then I began to question if the problem was really them or me. Naturally, my ego's first response was that it couldn't be me; after all, I had many years of Agile experience, whilst they had none.

And then it hit me; that precisely was the problem – I had many years of Agile experience, while they had none. And as a result of all that experience, I was trying to "sell" them Agile by using the latest Agile jargon. This is like a Star Trek fan explaining the science behind wormholes and the impact it has had on the evolution of Klingons (just writing that last line confused me – no offence to any Trekkie or Klingon readers). No wonder those poor clients and management couldn't make sense of what I was talking about. Their dazed eyes should have been a clue. And because they couldn't understand what I was talking about, they struggled to see how Agile practices would benefit them, hence they had no reason to change what they were doing. That's why it's important to communicate in a way your target audience can relate to and understand.

Because people have different learning styles (some are auditory and need to hear things; some are visual and need to see things; some are kinaesthetic and need to experience things), it is always a good idea, as well as tailoring your message to suit your audience, to also vary how that message is delivered.

For example, one of the methods I currently use to explain Agile is to first draw/show the familiar Waterfall delivery model (Figure 2 below).

Figure 2: Traditional Waterfall Model

Walking them through the model, I focus on the fact that 60% to 80% of development costs are associated with fixing the bugs identified during the testing stage and that because testing occurs so late in the development process, it often leads to projects running late and over budget. I then point out that even when all the bugs are fixed and the system is functioning as expected, because the customer rarely sees the end product till the final stage, there's always the risk that what is delivered is not what they were expecting, or will no longer meet their current needs, thereby resulting in failed projects.

Next I show them Figure 3 (below) and explain that with Agile projects, all we're doing is taking each phase of the traditional method and compressing them into smaller time periods, anywhere from 2 to 4 weeks that are repeated until the project objectives are achieved. I also emphasise that because the project is developed in phases, the customer benefits from:

- The ability to change their requirements, often at no extra cost, every two to four weeks in response to any changes in the market, economy, or their needs.
- Regular design reviews, resulting in more robust technical solutions due to growing domain knowledge and technological advancements.
- Higher quality of implementation as a result of the development team's experience and domain knowledge improving with each phase.
- Significant reductions in the cost associated with fixing defects because of early and regular testing.
- Quicker returns on investment as a result of new functionality being delivered and ready for use every two to four weeks.

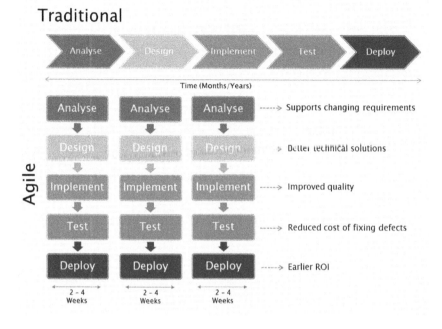

Figure 3: Agile Model

Using this audio-visual approach helps me explain the Agile software development process in simple terms without having to resort to jargon. And because it's presented in relation to a traditional model that your audience is likely to already be familiar with, it's much easier to understand.

From there, you can use simple terms to outline the minimum commitment needed from the customer in order to realise the benefits Agile has to offer; e.g., allocating a dedicated customer representative/product owner to act as the domain expert and highlight which features the business wants delivered first. And if you're in a workshop setting, you can also use some simple Agile games/exercises to give them an experiential based understanding of how Agile works in practice (there are loads of free Agile games/exercises with instructions on when and how to use them at TastyCupCakes.com and InnovationGames.com).

What I have outlined here is a jargon-free approach I currently use, with much success, to explain the Agile software development process. You are welcome to use it, too. But whatever approach you choose, make sure to explain Agile in simple terms that your audience will find easy to understand, because people rarely support things they do not understand.

CHAPTER 13

# Do This and You'll Have Everyone's Cooperation

*"No person, idea or institution becomes great until great resistance has been encountered. Greatness cannot be achieved until this concept is understood."*
**William Penn Patrick**

As you proceed with your Agile transition, the chances are you're going to experience a degree of resistance. That's to be expected because people are habitual and once they get used to doing something in a certain way, they are often reluctant to change. As a result, when people are introduced to something new, especially something they might not fully understand, it's not uncommon for them to display behaviour that can easily be considered as resistance. However, when we dig deeper, we sometimes find that what might appear to be resistance on the surface is, often, an expression of valid underlying concerns that have not been fully addressed yet.

And that's worth bearing in mind when introducing Agile into an organisation, because with change comes uncertainty, and uncertainty leads to concerns about how that change will impact the future. Some typical (often valid) concerns people have around Agile transition include:

- Is my job at risk?
- What if I can't do 'Agile'?
- How will the change affect my role/status?
- Will this create more work for me?
- If it all goes wrong, will I get the blame?

Typically our natural response to resistance is to try and overcome it by "pushing back" with logic and arguments in support of our position. But this often causes the other side to dig in and hold steadfast to their position. And as physics teaches us, opposing forces of equal strength cancel each other out.

An alternative, more productive approach to dealing with resistance would be to resolve it, which you do by addressing the other person's concerns; because, the truth is, people rarely resist change just for the sake of resisting. They usually have reasons, even if those reasons are valid only to them. And because people won't always say what their real reasons are for doing or not doing something, sometimes we have to delve deeper to unearth their true concerns. That's the reason why, in sales, objections are treated as requests for additional information; because professional salespeople know that the first few reasons a prospect gives for not moving forward with a purchase are often not their real reason. Therefore, each successful resolution of a "No" is seen as taking one step closer to a "Yes."

Resolution is an effective way to deal with resistance. You see, because people expect their resistance to be met with force they put their defences up. But showing an interest in a person's concerns lowers their defences and demonstrates that you care about what's important to them. In competitive working environments, that is a rare quality worth having, especially since people in such environments are used to everyone looking out for their own personal interests. But taking time out to genuinely understand and address a person's underlying concerns builds rapport and trust, earning you support as people start regarding you as someone who looks out for them.

However, in order for you to maintain that trust, you have to be honest and congruent at all times. Because, as previously stated, these techniques are not to be used for manipulation purposes. So if somebody is concerned that Agile transition will affect their role, don't tell them it won't if you know it will. Or if someone's afraid that they will not be able to grasp Agile practices, and you tell them you will support them through the transition, make sure you do.

Because the more congruency and integrity you have, the more people will want to listen, support, and readily be influenced by you.

CHAPTER 14

# The Key to Succeeding with Agile

*"The quality of an organization can never exceed the quality of the minds that make it up."*
**Harold R. McAlindon**

I don't know about you, but personally, I can't think of any software system or process that exists independently of people's input; even automated systems are designed, developed, and maintained by people. Likewise, although hammers are useful tools for building houses, I am yet to come across one that can wield itself without human effort.

That's because processes and tools in and of themselves don't do anything. It's people that execute/use them. That's not to say processes or tools are not important; they are. But people are just as, if not more, important because people make things happen. I guess that's why one of my earliest project managers used to say: *"Every project would be delivered on time and within budget; if it wasn't for the people."*

The Agile Manifesto value of *"individuals and interactions over processes and tools"* hints at the important role people play in achieving outcomes, and with good reason. At birth we need people's help coming into this world and then to feed, clothe, and protect us until we can do those things for ourselves. And when we die we're likely to need people to bury or cremate us, take care of our personal affairs, and do whatever else needs doing once we've passed on. So if we need people's help at the beginning and end of our lives, does it not make sense that we also need them throughout the duration of our lives? Especially since the things we want in life will always require another person's direct or indirect input because the truth is, people make things happen. Governments who recognise this fact tend to do well when they remember they're in power only by virtue of their people; whilst dictators who forget this often receive a rude awakening when their abuse of power causes their people to revolt against them.

This is a fact also worth remembering in regards to your Agile projects because Agile methodologies and tools do not achieve objectives; people do.

Something else worth bearing in mind is that as well as treating people as you'd like to be treated, it is also a good idea to treat them how they want to be treated – within reason, of course, especially since we all have different needs, and what works for one doesn't always work for others. Treating people how they want to be treated makes them feel good about themselves; and people who feel good about themselves tend to be more productive. Therefore, since effective, self-organising teams are essential to the success of Agile projects, it's in your best interest to nurture, support, and help your team members reach their full potential, especially as their combined skill sets, experience, and knowledge have the potential to create a wide range of solutions for your Agile projects.

The key to getting the most out of self-organising teams is belief and trust because good leaders know that belief in a person often inspires them to go above and beyond expectations. So as leaders, not only should we believe and trust that our teams can and will do what is required of them, we should also ensure that any process, methodology, or tool supports them in doing what they need to do.

And in the next chapter we'll be looking at a few things that will help us become better Agile managers and leaders.

CHAPTER 15

# Doing This Only Takes a Minute, but the Results Can Last a Lifetime

*"If your actions inspire others to dream more, learn more, do more and become more, you are a leader."*
**John Quincy Adams**

Have you read the bestselling book, *The One Minute Manager*? It's a short, easy read that demonstrates practical management techniques backed by several studies in medicine and behavioural sciences. According to the book there are "tough" managers whose organisations seem to win while their people lose; and there are "nice" managers whose people seem to win while the organisation loses. But effective managers are those who manage in such a way that both an organisation and its people benefit from each other's presence.

I don't know about you, but I do know that I've worked with tough managers whose only focus was to achieve objectives and hit targets. And because they were so results driven, they tended to crack-the-whip, micro-manage and command-and-control. In such instances, the business has tended to fare much better than the employees, who typically have been left feeling downtrodden, undervalued, and demotivated. I've also worked with nice managers who appeared to only be interested in pleasing the people working under them. And because they created laid-back environments where people came and went as they pleased and did what they wanted when they wanted, the business suffered as a result of deadlines not being met, poor quality deliverables, etc. I'm sure you'd agree that neither of these outcomes is desirable.

On Agile projects, the role of managers is seen as being very different from that on traditional projects. As effective Agile leaders, we should aim to create win-win situations that mutually benefit our organisation and the people working alongside or under us. So here are a few things that might help you achieve that objective:

> **Set Clear Goals and Expectations** – personally, I hate being in situations where it's not clear what I should be doing or what is expected of me. Maybe you do, too. If so, the chances are other people also feel the same, and that's why it's important that we give our teams clear goals and objectives to work towards. On Agile projects, requirements are typically documented as user stories supported by acceptance criteria and an agreed definition of "done". These are then communicated to the team so that everyone is clear on what needs to be done and what the expected end result looks like.

**Inspire & Motivate** – the happier and more content a person is, the better they perform. So as effective Agile leaders, we should aim to inspire and motivate our teams to be and do more. Inspiration is often thought of as a way of generating ideas, but it is much more than that. It is a powerful, driving force that motivates people to achieve given goals.

One way to inspire people is to believe and trust they will do what's required of them, because belief in a person[9] will often inspire them to go the extra mile and exceed expectations. That's not to say that everyone will live up to your trust. In fact, a small minority might even go as far as abusing it. But the majority will honour that trust and prove themselves worthy of it.

Another way to motivate people is by giving them meaningful and sometimes challenging work to do because people get bored with doing mundane, repetitive work. In contrast, meaningful, challenging work motivates and leads to a sense of pride, and with pride comes higher quality.

**Empower Them** – when people are empowered they feel confident, good about themselves and in control. You empower Agile teams by giving them the freedom to self-organise, letting them agree their own workload and choose how to implement technical solutions, free of external influence or micro-management. And although the

---

[9] If you ever find yourself struggling to believe in someone, remember that everyone is a potential winner; even those disguised as losers. So don't be fooled by appearances.

business can tell them what they want done, the team has the final say on how to do it. So as leaders, it's our responsibility to provide team members with a supportive environment and protect them from outside influences.

**Acknowledge Concerns and Feedback** – people like to be heard; it makes them feel valued. So it's important to acknowledge people's project concerns and consider their feedback when provided. In fact, one of the worst things you can do is totally ignore or disregard what a person has to say because that demoralises and causes them to shut down. But taking visible action to address their concerns or implement their feedback demonstrates that you value what they had to say, and that makes them feel good.

**Reward and Celebrate Successes** – in behavioural science, desired behaviours are created then reinforced using a reward system. At SeaWorld Orlando, for example, it's not unusual to see a killer whale or dolphin jump out of the water and over a rope, splashing anybody nearby. This is not something whales do naturally in the wild. They are taught it through a series of rewards (i.e., fish) received each time they elicit a response in line with the desired behaviour; e.g., when they cross a rope on the aquarium floor, swim over a rope suspended underwater, etc. Rewards are also an effective way for reinforcing human behaviour, and those rewards don't have to be anything extravagant. Simple things like acknowledgment, recognition, and celebrating team successes are often sufficient.

These are just a few of the things we can do to become effective managers and leaders. And even if you do not currently hold the title 'manager', the fact you're reading this right now means you are a change-agent who has what it takes to spearhead your organisation's Agile transition. And that makes you a leader.

Every leader has followers. But the question is: How do you ensure you have the right team behind you to achieve the desired end goal?

In the next chapter we'll be looking at what it takes to create highly productive Agile teams.

CHAPTER 16

# How to Build Effective Agile Teams

*"Teamwork is the ability to work together toward a common vision. The ability to direct individual accomplishments toward organizational objectives. It is the fuel that allows common people to attain uncommon results."*
**Andrew Carnegie**

Chances are you've heard of the United States Marine Corps, also known as the Marines, especially since they are one of the world's most formidable fighting forces. Experts at dealing with very complex, fast changing situations under any conditions, the Marines are also the ultimate Agile team. And because cross-functional, self-organising teams are fundamental to the success of Agile projects, here are a few things the Marines can teach us about creating effective teams that will help achieve those all-important victories you're after.

**Size Does Matter** – Believing that small, cross-functional units are the key to winning or losing battles, especially in complex, chaotic environments, Marine teams are made up of four to five riflemen, each likely to have different military specialities. Considering that a large number of Marine deployments currently take place within fast-changing, urban warfare environments, small units are ideal for maintaining visual contact and communication in situations when the field of view might be limited or radio signals blocked by urban terrain; i.e. buildings.

Based on the Agile principle that, *"the most efficient and effective method of conveying information to and within a development team is face-to-face conversation,"* it's advisable to also keep your Agile teams small (e.g., seven, plus or minus two on Scrum projects) because small teams collaborate better. You also want to ensure that your team is cross-functional, consisting of the skill-sets/roles relevant to your project objectives (e.g., Business Analyst, Developer, Tester, Front End Developer, etc). Bringing diverse skill-sets together in collaboration increases the quality of the end solution, reduces risk of making costly design or implementation mistakes, and enhances expertise through knowledge sharing.

**Skillset** – the Marines have a reputation for producing some of the best soldiers in the world. But the recruits don't start out like that; instead they are put through an intense training programme where they are assessed on a wide range of abilities and traits, including physical fitness, mental strength, leadership, honour, courage, and commitment.

Now, I'm not suggesting that you subject people to an intensive training programme, but you might want to select skilled or at least competent people for your Agile teams because they're the ones most likely to help you achieve the quick wins you need in the shortest time possible. Another reason for selecting skilled and competent team members is that in the early stages of your Agile transition you might not have the time required to nurture people unable to "hit the ground running".

**Team Dynamics** – although made up of individuals, Marine teams are moulded into a single, coherent unit bound together by mutual trust in each other, trust that their teams members will do what they are supposed to do, will cover their back at all times, and won't leave them behind if they were to fall in battle.

Although things can get hairy on Agile projects, fortunately the last thing your team members need to worry about is being left behind in battle. However, there still needs to be a degree of trust that team members will do what they say they will towards the achievement of the collective goal. Trust is reinforced through accountability, and that is part of the reason why during daily stand-up meetings popular within Scrum, team members share with each other what they did the day before and what they will be doing on the current day that will contribute to the collective objective. In doing so, they are being accountable to each other, and accountability is good for team dynamics.

Finally, make sure your pilot team members are all interested in trying a new way of working, and are not anti-Agile; because if they are, it will negatively impact the team dynamics and could cause your projects to fail.

**What, Not How** - To ensure every Marine has the ability, and authority, to make important decisions in the midst of chaos or in the absence of specific orders, Marines operate according to the philosophy of "Commander's Intent". Essentially, this means that when a subordinate leader finds himself in a situation where he needs to make an immediate decision, he has the basis for action that allows him to make the decision that best supports his commander's desired end state.[10] Put another way, Marine leadership focuses on WHAT to do (communicated through simple, unambiguous commands) and they leave the Marines to decide HOW to do it (the details) because leadership believes and trusts that their Marines have the right training and skillset to get the job done.

Similarly, on Agile projects, although the Product Owner or Customer might decide what requirements need to be delivered and in what order, it's the development team who decide how to implement those requirements because that's their area of speciality. That's why it's important that Agile teams are empowered to make decisions without external interruption or interference. Part of that empowerment involves trust and belief in your teams; trust that they have the skillset to implement the solution (if you've picked your team members right, that shouldn't be a consideration) and belief they will do what needs to be done when it needs doing.

---

[10] Marine Corps website: http://www.marines.com

**Plan Early, Plan Twice** – Marines don't plan too far ahead or in the absence of clear orders because unexpected twists or new developments might make the earlier planning irrelevant. They believe if you plan early, you're likely to plan twice.

The same holds true for the software development process where making irreversible technical decisions too early can prove very costly. According to authors of *Lean Software Development: An Agile Toolkit*, Mary and Tom Poppendieck, the most costly mistakes are made by forgetting to consider something important at the beginning; and the easiest way to make big mistakes is to drill down to detail too fast. So to avoid big mistakes and to eliminate waste on Agile projects, it's best to delay detailed decisions, especially design related ones, until the *last responsible moment;*[11] that is, the moment at which failing to make a decision eliminates an important alternative.[12] The key here is to defer risky decisions, individually or as a team, till as late as you responsibly can, because that's when you'll have the most information to make a decision upon, thereby significantly reducing the risk it will be the wrong one.

**Don't Aim For Perfection** – Understanding that even with the best laid plans things can still go wrong, Marines do

---

[11] Term coined by the Lean Construction Institute – see www.leanconstruction.org

[12] Mary and Tom Poppendieck, "Lean Software Development: An Agile Toolkit", 47-57

not strive for perfection. Instead they opt for solutions with a 70% chance of success because on the battlefield, speed and boldness are more important than perfection. Perceiving indecisiveness to be a fatal flaw, the Marines also believe it's better to make small decisions frequently because doing so provides quick feedback that can be used to create and execute better solutions in future.

Similarly, on Agile projects, planning and development are done iteratively, enabling teams to become more effective by quickly incorporating lessons learnt and feedback from earlier phases into subsequent ones. In this manner, over time Agile teams are able to deliver better quality solutions, improve their skills and gain more experience as they go along.

As you can see, the Marines "agility" enables them to respond quickly and effectively in fast-changing, complex, unpredictable, high-risk environments. And since software development projects tend to exist within fast-changing, complex, unpredictable, high-risk environments too, it makes sense to take a leaf out of the Marines' book when building effective Agile teams.

One of the dangers with letting teams self-organise is that if they misunderstand what's required of them, they might go off and develop the wrong thing. So in the next chapter we'll be looking at something simple you can do to prevent that happening on your projects.

CHAPTER 17

# How to Quickly Cut Through Red Tape and Avoid Frustrating Bureaucracy

*"Everything should be made as simple as possible, but not simpler."*
**Albert Einstein**

Have you heard this story about one of NASA's space programmes? It's the one where after a space mission NASA discovered that astronauts were unable to write in space because pens work by gravity pulling on the ink – and as you know, there's no gravity in space. To resolve this problem NASA invested millions of dollars creating a zero gravity pen that worked in space. However, the Russians came up with a different solution to the same problem: they gave their astronauts pencils.

Now, I'm not sure whether that story's true or just an urban legend, but either way it highlights the importance of keeping things simple, especially since people sometimes believe that good solutions have to be complicated.

Looking back at the Marines, we see that their "Commander's Intent" philosophy empowers soldiers to make their own decisions on how best to execute an order. And because they're not restricted by instructions telling them what to do, the Marines have the flexibility to choose from a number of available options, thereby enabling them to respond to any circumstance. For example, the order, *"Take building 'A' with minimum civilian casualties,"* clearly communicates the mission objective, also known as the "end state", thereby enabling the Marines to devise a plan on how to achieve that objective and then execute that plan in line with the Marines' core values. And once the mission is over, failure or success, they would report back as to what they did and why.

That's what we want to do on our Agile projects, too. We want to empower our development teams to make decisions based on newly available information, because they are the ones on the "front line", and therefore best positioned to address emerging issues or take advantage of new opportunities as and when they arise. So if we want the ability to respond quickly in today's fast-changing, competitive marketplaces, we need to enable our teams to make decisions without being restricted by bureaucracy or red tape.

Now, I don't know about you, but in the past I've worked on projects where the team wasn't empowered to respond to newly emerging opportunities or issues. And because the "decision makers" would take a long time to decide how best to respond to the situation, time, money, and resources were often wasted in waiting for a decision to be made. And when they finally did make a decision, it usually came too late for the team to act upon. So to avoid waste, reduce the cost of development, and minimise risk we need to give our teams simple rules that will guide their decision making process.

Simple rules are outcome driven, decision-making frameworks and, unlike instructions, they're not context specific, therefore providing flexibility under a wide range of situations – a bit like a debit or credit card. In today's global economy, a debit or a credit card can be used in many countries around the world. You can travel to most places on the globe and still use your card to complete a purchase or withdraw cash, regardless of the card's country of origin. On the other hand, you're likely to be limited in the number of places around the world where you can spend your local currency.

Just as the Marines' decision-making process and actions are guided by simple rules in the form of their core values, we also need to provide our teams with simple rules that give them the flexibility to quickly respond, in line with the project objectives, to changing circumstances; be they newly emerging opportunities or issues.

But even with simple rules in place, there's still a possibility that things might not go to plan. And if that does happen, how do you deal with it? Read on to find out.

CHAPTER 18

# What to Do When Things Go Wrong

*"Remember the two benefits of failure. First, if you do fail, you learn what doesn't work; and second, the failure gives you the opportunity to try a new approach."*
**Roger von Oech**

Have you ever wondered why some people have a strong fear of failure? Maybe the roots of that fear can be traced back to early childhood when they might have been criticised or given a look of disappointment by well-meaning parents for doing something wrong. And because every child craves parental approval, they stopped trying new things for fear of risking further disproval. Or maybe the whole class laughed at them when they got a question wrong, and because no one likes being made to look stupid (especially in public) the fear of being ridiculed caused them to play it safe and stay within their comfort zone in future situations.

Over time, we all develop self-limiting beliefs that have the potential to trap us in a comfort zone that restricts our full potential. And pretty soon those beliefs slip into our sub-conscious, determining what we think we can and cannot do.

When circumstances or fear of failure stop us from trying new or different things, we are often left feeling unhappy or unsatisfied. Maybe you know people right now who are unhappy with their relationship, job, or financial situation, but because changing things requires them to venture outside their comfort zone, they stick with what they know, hoping things will eventually get better by themselves. But, according to Albert Einstein, *"doing the same thing over and over again and expecting different results"* is insane.

However you look at it, the reality is that failure is a necessary part of life. It's a process we all have to undergo if we want to grow and get better at anything. Think about it, at the time of writing this, I have a sixteen-month-old son who started walking just before his 1$^{st}$ birthday. But before he learnt how to walk on his own, he fell over countless times. He would stand up, fall down, stand up, fall down; take one step, fall over; take 2 steps, fall over; take 3 steps, fall over again and again and again until he finally learnt how to walk confidently.

The chances are you went through a similar process when you were learning how to walk too, but imagine for one second what would have happened if after the first time we fell down we decided not to try again? We'd still be crawling around on all fours. However, because we had no perception of failure at that point in our lives, we persisted until we finally got it right. We stepped, no pun intended, outside our comfort zone in fearless pursuit of what we wanted. Believing that people thrive under adversity and challenges, Marine officers reward failure because not only is the occasional failure seen as a sign that a Marine is pushing beyond their comfort zone, they also believe it's the best learning experience. This view is also shared by Bill Gates, the richest man in the world for 13 straight years, who said, *"It's fine to celebrate success, but it is more important to heed the lessons of failure."*

So how is all this relevant to your Agile projects?

Well, firstly it's important you are aware that things might not go as planned when you first start using Agile practices. In fact, productivity is likely to drop initially as you and your team undergo the learning curve associated with working in this new way. And if that does happen, know that it's OK, because the iterative approach adopted by Agile practices enables us to learn and adapt throughout the development process. Secondly, because software and product development are about creating solutions to unsolved problems, there's a good chance some mistakes will be made along the way. Recognising this fact, the Agile development lifecycle includes end of iteration retrospectives and reviews that enable us to learn from our mistakes so we can avoid them in future.

It is important to understand that there are two types of failure: temporary and permanent. The former is a learning experience, while the latter is "game over". And the key to eliminating the possibility of permanent failure is persistence ... because you can't fail if you never give up. Think about it; it took Thomas Edison over 10,000 attempts to invent the light bulb in common use today. But when asked how he managed to keep going after so many failures Edison replied, *"I have not failed. I just found 10,000 ways that won't work."* Now, I'm not suggesting you pursue Agile transition with that degree of persistence (although, hat off to you if you possess that rare level of tenacity) but what I am saying is that if you truly believe Agile will benefit you and your organisation, persistence will help you overcome obstacles, resolve resistance and address most of the issues you are likely to encounter along the way.

And if right now you're wondering how long it will take for your Agile transition to yield the results you're after, you'll find the answer in the next chapter.

CHAPTER 19

# A Rule of Thumb Worth Bearing in Mind

*"No great thing is created suddenly."*
**Epictetus**

Growing up I was very impatient, so much so that I was constantly looking for quick ways to learn patience. Needless to say I never found one, but I did learn patience . . . eventually.

Looking around, it's not hard to see why people might be impatient. Especially when you consider the fact that today's 'fast paced' culture encourages instant gratification in the form of coffee, credit cards, buy-now-pay-later schemes, and liposuction. Even technology supports instant gratification. For example, where years ago it could take months for a letter sent from one side of the world to reach a recipient on the other side, today people on different sides of the world can communicate in almost real time using electronic means, such as email, text, or instant messenger. And now that people have gotten used to having their desires immediately satisfied, it's no surprise they no longer want to wait for things. But taking a closer look, we'll see that instant results are not the natural order of things.

When farmers plant their crops they don't expect to harvest them the next day. Take apple trees, for example. Planted as a seedling they generally take a couple of years to get established in the ground and anywhere from six to ten years to bear fruit. But understanding that everything has its season, the farmer nurtures the tree over those years until it's ready to harvest.

Similarly, with Agile transition we need to plant the seeds of change and nurture them through to growth because organisational change rarely happens overnight. In fact, depending on the size and culture of the organisation, sometimes it can take years. Therefore a rule of thumb worth bearing in mind is that the longer an organisation has been doing things in a particular way, the longer it is likely to take them to change. Other factors that might also impact the speed of change within an organisation include economic climate, market conditions, and the political environment.

Knowing all this, it's important not to lose hope if your Agile transition appears to come up against a brick wall or is taking longer than you originally anticipated. Instead, be patient, persist, and hang-in-there, all the while understanding that although the seeds of change you've planted, or intend to, might not sprout straightaway, that doesn't mean they're not taking root, even if those roots are not yet visible. So during the early stages it's important to keep nurturing those roots until they yield the results you're after.

That said, just as some soil and environmental conditions are not conducive to the growth of certain crops, Agile transition might struggle to establish roots in organisations where the internal politics and cultural environment do not support change. In such environments the chances are that no matter what you say or do to demonstrate how a transition to Agile is in the organisation's best interest, it's likely to fall on deaf ears.

Similarly, Agile transition rarely succeeds in organisations with strong blame cultures because in those types of organisations people rarely make decisions for fear of making the wrong one. In this way, blame cultures stifle innovation and hinder change by preventing people from exploring or trying new things. Faced with these situations, patience is unlikely to produce the results you desire, in which case it might be worth asking yourself whether you really want to be working in a place that limits your potential and impedes your personal growth, because as Warren Buffet once said, *"Should you find yourself in a chronically leaking boat, energy devoted to changing vessels is likely to be more productive than energy devoted to patching leaks."*

At this point you might be wondering how best to move forward with all the transition techniques and strategies covered in this book, in which case, you might want to read the next chapter because it answers that question.

# What You Need to Know about Agile Best Practices

*"What works for one person may not work for another."*
**Jeffrey Lieberman**

Question: What is the best way to have and maintain a healthy, loving relationship where both party's needs are met at all times?

When I ask that question in my workshops and seminars I tend to get a wide range of different answers typically based on people's personal experience and what they've read or heard somewhere else. But through individual and group discussions they usually find out that something that might have produced the desired results for them (or someone they know) produced undesirable results for others because the fact is, what holds true for one person doesn't necessarily hold true for another.

That's something worth remembering when it comes to Agile best practices because best practices are often contextual and situational dependent, therefore they do not always hold true in every situation. In other words, one cap does not fit all.

Don't get me wrong, when first starting out with Agile practices it's advisable to stick as close as possible to the prescribed processes of your chosen methodology. But once you and your team are fully confident in using that methodology, it's okay to adapt it to suit your specific organisational and project needs. That's because Agile methodologies are not intended to be restrictive but rather to provide you with a framework (simple rules) within which to operate. Understanding the principles underlying the processes will give you the flexibility to adapt and respond to a wider range of situations. Therefore, it's worth viewing processes as guidelines rather than best practices.

When speaking at conferences, during the questions and answer section, people often ask me what they should do to address various issues specific to their organisation or project. When faced with such questions, I am always transparent in letting them know that I'm unable to give informed answers without understanding the full context of the issue, including organisational size, culture, political environment, maturity in using Agile methods, drivers, etc. And even then, the chances are, I would be able to make a suggestion based only on what might have worked for me or others faced with similar issues in the past, because every situation is different.

Take the contents of this book, for example. Are they guaranteed solutions to every problem that anyone might face with Agile transition? Maybe not, but they are guidelines. And because they are based on my personal experience and the experience of top Agile experts and thought leaders that I've been fortunate to interview and be mentored by over the years, these guidelines are likely to help you find solutions specific to your situation.

In my experience, the key to getting the most out of best practices is being able to extract what is relevant to your situation and then experimenting with it until you find what works best for you. This is because in reality we can get only so much from theory and reading books; the real discovery and value comes out of the practical application of what we learn. That's why it's important to change our perspective on failure and avoid a blame culture.

Being aware that best practices are not always best for everyone, you might want to use them as guidelines. And if something isn't working for you, don't be afraid to tweak it to better suit your specific needs, which brings us neatly onto the next chapter.

# The Oak and the Reed

*"Instead of striving to be right at a high cost, it will be more appropriate to be flexible and plural at a lower cost. If you cannot accurately predict the future then you must flexibly be prepared to deal with various possible futures."*

**Edward de Bono**

Have you heard of Mr Fantastic? He was the leader of the Fantastic Four superhero team, and his special powers enabled him to stretch his body into incredible lengths and shapes. In other words, he was flexible.

Speaking of flexibility, the dictionary defines the word 'agile' as being *"able to move quickly and easily."* [13] Looking at the Agile Manifesto, we also see that great value is placed on *"responding to change over following a plan"* – and for good reason too, because things don't always go as planned. In fast paced, dynamic environments, flexibility is often essential to project success, hence why so many organisations are now transitioning from Waterfall to Agile practices. Based on the assumption that everything about a project can be known and fully understood upfront, Waterfall projects tend to be driven

---

[13] Online Oxford Dictionaries: http://oxforddictionaries.com/definition/agile

by structured plans that attempt to maintain control by restricting change. However, this approach rarely works in practise, a fact evident from the high proportion of Waterfall projects that run over budget and time. Recognising that in the real world, needs and requirements do change and it's impossible to know everything upfront – especially since we don't know what we don't know – change is factored into Agile practices.

Over the last few years we've seen small, newly emerging companies successfully compete with, and even outdo, larger, well established companies, even though the larger companies usually have more resources and money than the smaller ones. One of the reasons for this is because smaller companies tend to be more flexible; often they can respond to market changes and technical advancements much quicker than larger companies. Objectives help us respond effectively to change because although being flexible might sometimes require us to abandon existing plans and venture into the unknown, objectives help ensure we don't lose our way – a bit like the North Star guiding sailors home.

In today's competitive, fast paced business world, speed is essential, especially since it can influence the buying decisions of people accustomed to instant gratification. Speed is also an important consideration for companies that want to do well during financially turbulent times because when cash flow is tight a company's survival often hinges on the speed at which it can realise returns on its investments. Agile projects address these needs by delivering working software early and frequently, thereby providing a quicker return on investment through the early utilisation of new functionality.

As we come to the end of this chapter, let me leave you with the following fable from the early Greek writer, Aesop:

*"An oak and a reed were arguing about their strength. When a strong wind came up, the reed avoided being uprooted by bending and leaning with the gusts of wind. But the oak stood firm and was torn up by the roots."*

Although this story is over 2,000 years old, its lessons still hold true today. So remember to be flexible, respond quickly to change, and adapt to circumstance because that's the key to success with Agile.

Speaking of success, there's one last thing you need to know that is fundamental to the success of all Agile projects . . . and you'll find that information in the following chapter.

CHAPTER 22

# The Truth about Agile

> *"There is at least one point in the history of any company when you have to change dramatically to rise to the next level of performance. Miss that moment, and you start to decline."*
>
> **Andy Grove**

As any driver will tell you, learning to drive takes a lot of concentration because as a learner, you have to consciously think about everything you need to do to get a car from A to B. I remember when I was first started learning how to drive. I would nervously get behind the wheel, check the gear was in neutral, start the engine, hold the steering wheel tight with both hands positioned at quarter-to-three, check my mirrors ten or more times, put one foot on the brake, press down on the clutch, take one hand nervously off the steering wheel, change gear, put hand back on steering wheel, etc. Then after all that, I'd end up stalling the car and would have to start the whole process again. And when I finally did get the car moving, I would end up creating a traffic jam by driving at 5 miles per hour in a 40 miles per hour area.

But now that I've have been driving for a while, I no longer have to consciously think about all the things involved in driving a car from A to B. I just do them automatically. Now I can confidently drive under a wide range of conditions (driving on the left not included) and often find myself instinctively responding to potentially life threatening situations before I'm even consciously aware of the danger.

In many ways, this also describes the subtle difference between "doing" and "being" Agile. "Doing Agile" is about consciously going through the motions and sequentially executing a prescribed set of practices. 'Being Agile', on the other hand, is about understanding and embracing the Agile principles and applying them to what we do. See, that's the thing about principles – they're universal, timeless, and self-evident. Unlike practices that might work in one situation but not necessarily in another, principles are universally applicable, and once internalised they empower us to create a wide variety of practises to deal with different situations.

Because software and product development tend to be complex, dynamic processes, it's important to remember that no single methodology can cover every possible eventuality; they each have their pros and cons. However, "being" Agile and principle driven enables you to maximise the pros and minimise the cons by drawing from different Agile methodologies, thereby giving you the flexibility to respond to a wider range of situations and issues.

That's something worth remembering because the wide-ranging problems people encounter with Agile transition and implementation make it impossible for a single book to provide *the solution* to every possible situation. However, books like this give you principles that will help you find solutions to your own specific problems. And considering the fact that software and product development are about finding solutions to existing problems, the ability to solve a wide range of problems is a skill definitely worth having – especially during times of uncertainty. For that reason, in return for creating solutions that result in organisations saving large amounts of money, and significantly increasing profits or achieving key business objectives, you as a problem solver can expect to enjoy greater job security, receive quicker promotions, and get paid more.

And I'm sure you'll agree that's as good a reason as any for "Being Agile".

## CHAPTER 23

# The Bigger Picture

*"You are here in order to enable the world to live more amply, with greater vision, with a finer spirit of hope and achievement. You are here to enrich the world."*
**Woodrow Wilson**

Creating change isn't easy, especially when that change is inspired by new ideas contrary to the way "things have always been done." And, unfortunately, the fact that the change might be beneficial to all doesn't always make the process any easier. Even so, we shouldn't shy away from leading change just because it might prove hard. Instead, like a plumber, we should arm ourselves with the right tools to get the job done.

Over the last twenty-two chapters you have learnt techniques and strategies some of the world's leading Agile experts use to successfully transition organisations from Waterfall to Agile practices. Pragmatic and cost effective, these proven techniques and strategies work – but only if you work them. Some of this information might not be new to you, and some of it will be. Either way, it's important to be aware that knowledge is power only when put into action; because to learn and not to do is really not to learn, and to know and not to do is really not to know. So start using this toolbox of information straight away, remembering it's a learning process based on continuous improvement. And go easy on yourself if things don't immediately turn out as expected. They will improve.

The most common reason for transitioning to Agile practices is to improve the software and product development process. So if there's value in improving processes that produce inanimate objects, then surely there's even greater value in improving ourselves so that we can be happier and more fulfilled in all areas of our lives, including our jobs, relationships, finances, health, etc?

Maybe you're tired of having "too much month at the end of the money" and struggling financially. Maybe you want to enjoy the level of confidence and happiness you've always dreamed of. Maybe you're ready to live life to the fullest, on your terms and not dictated by the economy, your boss, or other people's opinions. Maybe you're ready to have greater job security, get promoted quicker and be paid more. If so, then maybe Agile is for you. Because the truth is, Agile is more than a set of methodologies and processes; it's a philosophy and mind-set that extends beyond software and product development. It's a way of life that empowers people to be, do, and have more.

You see, over the years of interviewing Agile experts and thought leaders, I've been fortunate to meet people who have been using Agile practices with great success in a wide variety of areas including politics, social engagement, education, personal relationships, at home, financially. . . the list goes on.

And as a result, I now share the mission of those using Agile not just to improve the software and product development processes, but to also to improve individual lives and make the world a better place.

Yes, you should use the information in this book to transition your organisation from Waterfall to Agile practices, creating greater job security, quicker promotions, and earning more money for yourself in the process. And hopefully, because you can see that the strategies and techniques covered in this book are also relevant to life, you'll use them to create more happiness for yourself, have greater peace of mind and be even more fulfilled in all areas of your life – because happy fulfilled people positively impact others.

I'm reminded of a story about a CEO of a multi-national company who, whilst receiving a life-time achievement award at a company event, shared a story from his childhood. Back then he didn't have any friends, was a victim of constant bullying, and felt all alone. One day, after an intense day of bullying at school, on his way home the bullies set on him again, pushing him into a puddle and throwing his books on the wet ground. With tears in his eyes, he was picking up his books when a stranger walking by stopped, gave him a smile, bent down, helped him pick up the books and then gave him another smile before leaving. Taking a moment to hold back the tears, the CEO then went on to say that the stranger was the only reason why he was standing before them collecting that award, because on the day of that incident, he was actually on his way home to commit suicide. But that stranger's smile and actions had restored his faith in people's kindness, giving him hope for the future, and the personal drive that resulted in him winning the award he was receiving that day.

What this story demonstrates is that it doesn't take much to make a positive difference in another person's life. And when our own emotional, financial, social, and personal needs have been met, we are more likely to do the things that will positively impact other people's lives, thereby creating a positive, "butterfly effect"[14] that has the potential to impact the lives of people we might never come in direct contact with. A wise man once told me that in life, we should aim to first work on improving ourselves, then work on improving things for our families, then our friends, our community, our country, our race, and then – if we're able to – the whole human race because that's a legacy worth living for. Imagine for a moment what life would be like if more of us worked towards mutually beneficial goals. Wouldn't it be a much better world for our loved ones to live in?

That's the vision that motivates me.

Maybe you share a similar vision, too. Maybe you also want to live in a world with fewer wars, less violence, and greater regional and economic stability. . . a world where people's lives are valued regardless of who they are or where they come

---

[14] A phenomenon whereby a small change at one place in a complex system can have large effects elsewhere

from. . . a world where everyone feels like they have a stake in their communities and countries.

If so, then I'd be honoured to collaborate with you on that journey because one fist is much stronger than five fingers. And in memory of the late Steve Jobs (a man who had a vision of making the world a better place through technology), let me leave you with the following words: *"Stay Young, Stay Foolish!"*

**Stay Agile!**

# About the Author

Known as "The Agile Agilist," Ade Shokoya is the creator of the 'Agile Transition System' and founder of www.AgileTV.co.uk.

An Agile Business Analyst, ScrumMaster and Agile Consultant, Ade Shokoya specialises in delivering multi-million pound Agile projects and helping organisations gain a competitive advantage by transitioning from traditional methods to Agile practices. With over 10 years' experience gained from working on projects for internationally recognised brands (including Metro Newspaper, LexisNexis, Tesco and Capita), Ade Shokoya adopts a **K.I.S.S** (Keep It Simple & Straightforward) approach to Agile transition.

Author, radio talk show host, and public speaker, Ade regularly interviews the world's top Agile experts, including Arie van Bennekum (early DSDM adopter and Agile Manifesto author), Jeff Sutherland (Scrum co-creator & Agile Manifesto author), Ron Jefferies (XP creator and Agile Manifesto author), Jeff Patton (story mapping pioneer), Mary & Tom Poppendieck (lean software development pioneers), and many more.

A loving partner and father, Ade Shokoya supports a number of national and international charities.

*To create an Agile transition plan specific to your organisational needs, to have Ade Shokoya speak at your company/event, or to find out more about Ade's consultation services, please call +44 (0)8450 536 745, or go to www.AgileTV.co.uk*